The Picnic

in the Sky

Written by Diana Noonan   Illustrated by Clive Taylor

"We are too heavy," said Elephant. So she tossed out her hay.

3

"We are too heavy," said Bear.
So she tossed out her honey.

"We are too heavy," said Hippo.
So she tossed out her cabbages.

6

"We are too heavy,"
said Monkey.
So she tossed out
her bananas.

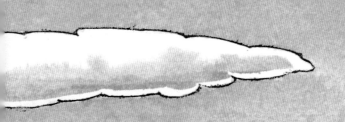

"We are too heavy," said Mouse. So she tossed out her cheese.

They went up and up and up.

"We are hungry," they said.
So they went down
and down and down.

12